The Language Creatures

ISOBEL THRILLING

The Language Creatures

Shearsman Books
Exeter

Published in the United Kingdom in 2007 by
Shearsman Books Ltd
58 Velwell Road
Exeter EX4 4LD

www.shearsman.com

ISBN-13   978-1-907500-21-9

ISBN-10   1-907500-21-0

Acknowledgements
Some of these poems have previously appeared in the following
publications. Thanks to the editors and judges concerned:
*East Anglian Poetry Competition Anthology, Essex Poetry Competition Anthology,
Exeter Poetry Competition Anthology, Frogmore Papers, A.E. Housman Memorial
Poetry Anthology, Images of Women* (ed. Myra Schneider & Dilys Wood, Ar-
rowhead Press, in association with Second Light, 2006); *Interpreter's House,
Journal of the Birmingham & Midland Institute Library, Orbis, Other Poetry,
Second Light, Suffolk Crabbe Memorial Poetry Anthology, The Lion Christian Po-
etry Anthology, Wymondham Poetry Competition Anthology.*

A number of the poems included in this volume have been awarded prizes;
details of these are given on page 87, in the continuation of this Acknowl-
edgements page.

The publisher gratefully acknowledges financial assistance with its 2005-2007
publishing programme from Arts Council England.

Contents

To my husband,
who has given me love and support over many years

The Amber Shop

When greyness becomes a wolf at my door,
I remember the amber shop
set in the washed-out blues and whites
of a crumbling east coast town.

Preserved sunlight: the amber is pale lemon
through to dark cinnamon,
stored afternoons from cretaceous times,
ancient radiances made solid
and carved
into necklaces, animals and fruit,
the colours of marmalade
and butterscotch,
apricot, mango, gold and peach,
nasturtium, wallflowers, primrose, ginger.

People absorb its terra-cotta rays,
surely their blood is charged with fires,
its essences, its vegetable lamps,
imprints from antique forests, staves of leaves.

A substance light and almost warm
to the touch, a living thing
transmuted with all its sugars and chemistries,
distillations from sky and earth.
Who could want gold or other metals
when they could
wear this murmurous cargo?

We are all pieces of amber,
the universe re-made running through our veins.

The Saxon Lyre

It lay near the sea at Prittlewell
in a prince's grave
with the folding-chair and vases,
armour and sword;

the ghost of a lyre.

Its broken,
wooden pieces linked by stains
in the soil
created the ancient shape,

shadow-music.

Ravens of grief
still hang
in the grey and silver landscape.
Did warriors
sound the precious metals
of lament,
clashing their weapons
in despair and celebration?

Most touching are the repairs,
the delicate gold
and silver
rivets worked with precision,
the handmade nails.

Long plank of wood,
strings joined at one smooth end,
fanned like
the wing of a bird,

it preserves
the reverence of hands.

Reconstructed,
an echo of shells in the notes,
once again, it weaves
its bones into the cadences of men.

The Singing Bowl

I hadn't known of the Tibetan
singing bowl;

once told,
it haunts my head.

Echoes
from peaks, stars, snows,
high, sweet blade
of frost
or thrum from copper sun
roll through
its strung substance,

hollowed stone, spun clay
or mineral dish
with shimmer and hum.

A note
with feathered edges
like silk
or full as the moon
slipping metals into the lake?

Spinets and samisens spill
along axons,

a lute, a harp, a gong,
a bell;

cup of sound to hold the world.

Birth of an Escapologist

This bowl of hyacinths transmits
a blue pulse,
scent heavy with thunders,

a bruise,
a thug at the throat,
the child is drugged with boredom,
slugged by sweetness.

The afternoon
swings its cosh and elderly aunts,
avid yet powdery,
flutter their bones, ecstatic
among the tea-cups,
sleeves rustle like membranes.

She has lost the power to hear
their voices,
just a needle of sound can stab
the silence
wound round her head;
the air wraps her in hot velvet.

She is living a fairy-tale,
the chrysalis of a child in thrall,
she must weave
her own colours, make inner fabric.

Wings of curtains drift over
this new creature
assembling its natal flight,
the skill to release herself to the sky.

The Language Creatures

Some words are satisfying as good tools,
those for artefacts,
terms for things we do.

They give a solid heft on the world,
we love their grip,
they help us brew and build and shape.

Other words are tenuous, half-seen
they glint at parties,
prowl through committee, business, bank,
fabled beasts,
at one with the gryphon, unicorn, gorgon.

Most fearsome is when tongues
fail completely,
we sense amorphous wraiths,
qualms, sensations, terrors
that carry no title,
(not fish, nor fowl, nor good, red herring).

Not all are perilous, some flicker
suspended radiance,
imprints, intimations beyond
the reach encoded in genes or neurons.

All language trails the weight
of a trackless deep,
where creatures wait to be born, given a name.

Before Lazarus

Leopard: dark firework undetected
by the impala,
slips through ebony, mahogany,
thick night alive with jasmine.

Invisible lamp:
brain igniting filaments in nerve
and tendon, unloosing fibres
in jaw and paw.

Her leap assembles.

A velvet hunting-equation with
claws and teeth, a piece
of physics written in language
of the cosmos;

the furring of maths.

Such translations, shape-shifts
in the firmament,
strange as Greek myths,
are never perceived as miracles.

Kin to stars, we, too,
are the old din of the universe.
Blood, lava, bone and clay evolved

from a chunk of sun,
we are the planet given a voice,
clunch of grief and love.

Electrons in stones are the same
as those in a human head,
we are sky
and reassembled time,
life is a metamorphosis of death.

We were raised from the dead.

Tracking the Gold Frog

Dusk clings to shoes and clothes
marooning faces
to float like balloons,
footless we come down the hill.

Lizzie picks up trails of leaves,
collects them like
footprints from huge, gold frogs.
Aged three, she does not
know what tracks the world,
unicorns are as likely as birds,
woolly mammoths
could raise their heads at a zoo.

Medieval chemists never turned
lead into gold,
yet the earth achieves a deeper
alchemy with trees,
armadillos, nightingales and Lizzie.

We, too, follow tracks in the cosmos,
astral paths, great beasts of light.
Angels could flow natural
as electricity, hidden shoals.
Deep physics
with its other dimensions,
illumines the grain of imagination,

opens space in
the firmament, where the spirit can go.

Anonymous Caller

Like Hamlet's uncle, drops poison in one ear,
face like candy, hard as peppermint rock,
she glitters with venomous virtue, brittle fear.

Sharp, little smiles bite open her mouth, she veers
towards righteousness, delivers a shock
like Hamlet's uncle. Drops poison in one ear.

In co-ordinated colours, she stands out clear
as frost, in matching earrings, bracelet, frock.
She glitters. With venomous virtue, brittle fear,

she creates a ghost, believes she is sincere.
Dissembling her voice, she puts it under a lock
like Hamlet's uncle. Drops poison in one ear.

She loves the delicate bristles that will appear
in someone's frightened tone. They hear her mock.
She glitters with venomous virtue. Brittle fear

has made her into a victim compelled to sneer
at those unlike herself, not of her flock.
Like Hamlet's uncle, drops poison in one ear.
She glitters with venomous virtue, brittle fear.

A Kind of Mugging

A sense of varnish, coating
for the psyche,
glittering tintinnabulations
of gold and scarlet.

Lulled by fibrous warmth
in her voice,
bee-burr with honey,
you feel safe.

Impressively white-toothed,
she smiles,
adept at being pleasantly
disobliging,
creates a fairground effect,
the ground migrates,
dislocating as first-stage migraine.

In Imitation of Eden

Red face, dark ears, a Mickey Mouse
plant at Eden in Cornwall
shocks like a miracle,
a cartoon growth in the Garden.

She remembers Kew,
how the scent of lilac rolled
its purple smoke,
they met seed-heads fierce as angels,
pitcher-plants
each in its own green hell.

Such places are always biblical,
green sky, vegetable velvet,
flowers cut from fabric
thick as felt,
strong enough for a coat.

Ghosts of buildings,
half-visible ribs against clouds,
walls caught
in the act of a haunting
echo their own sense of substance,
women with camouflage,
who could fade into any furniture,
at one with Regency stripe,
or floral design
on silk, chintz or uncut moquette.

They loved this flamboyant growth,
exotic excess,
it made them at ease with their
own cultivations,
asphodels, moonflowers, lilies of myth.

Aquarium

O   Fish:

pale amethyst,

quilted moons adrift

O   behind glass. Little cushions

tasselled and fringed with fins.

O   Chandeliers pendant in water, their

O   sway **0**))   precarious as treasure-ships,

a list to port or starboard could let slip the ballast of

light. We imitate their skin despite the deep with

its dark shapes, trail scarves and filaments,

sequins for scales, flights of fronds and

drapery. At parties, sculling in

radiant shoals, we browse

our own sunlit

reefs.

Variations on a Theme

In hospital, pain is graded on a scale
'slight to moderate, severe to excruciating'

Within two days I'm off to wash toting
my drainage-tube,
small bucket of blood, bar of soap;

to walk is a fine tune.

I learn orchestrations, movements,
how to mute
muscle-beat, blare, a blizzard of strings,
certain rhythms are gold.

It helps to arrange the body like clay
assembling a sculpture,
materialise round pain, adapt to its shape.

Soft-pedalling opiates disturb the world,
I diminish their tone,
at times, I prefer pure noise.

Every day there's a change in key,
subtle variations.
It's odd the way pain can jangle
life's phrases,
dislocate angles in someone's smile,

change voices in a landscape,
disrupt the geology under a conversation.

I recall a child who craved
a kind word more
than a sweet — I devour the same cadence.

Honed

Houses lodged under cliffs among
limpets and whelks,

a place with its own cadences;

struck rock,
gulls born swinging each cry
like an axe,
elementals adept at assessing
the chainmail of stones.

Children catch sky in pails,
pieces of cloud,
little, green crabs,

keep pebbles as pets.

I watch sea dissolving pearls:
in winter, waves
break over the 'Cod and Lobster'.

Above my head
birds cut invisible contours
with quills,
the topography of flying,
hidden worlds
mapped with a coded script.

After cancer, gutted and cured,
I can pause with
these people hewn to life on the edge.

Growing the Season

I have put away my summer kimono,
(gift from my daughter),
folded its petals and wings,
silk blossom,
the long-necked cranes
settle coolly into the cedar box.

Late August: the rains are early,
the apples are down.
Yesterday we packed their green skin
into wicker-work baskets.

September disintegrates into wefts,
bright lion-winds, gold raging,
leaves breaking
under the weight of sky.

This spring was my time for red silts,
ebb-tides in the blood,
scalpels and wounds.
Body stripped to its wires,
old griefs showed unfamiliar faces.

In the ward, the windows were
too high to reach,
tall foliage swelled into green sails.
I knew then, the psyche
grows seeds to reflect an internal season.

Conjurations

I loved you for glimmerings and hauntings,
the northern hills in your head,
ships' rigging etched in your cells.

Liverpool was luminous, patches of sky
slipping from streets, roofs,
light loosed, as rain
released its silver tarnishings.

You dragged ghosts from Ireland,
Bootle was harsh,
yet the Mersey ran with stars,
you were moored to dreams.

We only met once in your city,
its sails in my head
among the ruins of our silences.

I couldn't stay with your mists,
hint of the Ancient Mariner in your bones,
the fear you would turn me
into the phantom of what I might have been.

Love Poem

The need to see you
is a knot of pain lodged
underneath the ribs.

I craved the delight
of a light flirtation.

Now, like Prometheus,
who stole fire,
I'm devoured daily;
not just liver,

heart and bones and skin.

Assembling the Yarn

Needles are pathfinders, rein fantasy animals,
red, orange, splodged purple, pink,
they pull towards oases
in her head;
wool-beasts leap into her lap.

She has salvaged yarns from scarves,
jackets, hats, unravelling
the family's history re-weaves fibres
from grandmother's tales,
great aunt's whispering cardigan,
cuffs from gloves,
shades from a fabled waistcoat.

Lost library in wool waits in the wardrobe;
mingled greys from winter bloom
in her hands, white shadows
edged in ash, garment
of ghosts, absences, weft of wraiths.

No snippet is discarded, one row of stitches
creates a flick in the fabric,
recalls how granddad, woollen-cables
slung over his back,
dug a door in the architraves of snow.

She works ancestral threads through days,
great-grandmother let loose,
amok among coloured hanks, knitting her story.

Making the Scarf

A yarn ripe with the colours
of raspberries,
brambles and sloes,

surely, the juices
will stain my hands?

I think about
wines and summer pudding.

I could have knitted
dragon's breath,
long, flaring fibres in flame
and red,
undertow in umber.

A token of love,
it's a time for comfort.
I choose to loop my script
in inks from
hedgerows and wild fruit,

left exotic
creatures asleep on the shelves.

Woman Knitting

Hours made visible, a purple mist
flows from her hands,
shawls of shadows, accumulation
of twilight,
moments looped
with dusks and glimmerings.

Thread, harsher, stronger
rubs thumb.
She is patched with plasters,
knitting up days,
weeks, griefs, anxieties,
unravelling viscera, stitching red.

Fabric stretches to the horizon,
she is hooking up moons
and radiances, the inner landscape;
all day the needles
are clicking their little hooves,
travelling . . . travelling . . .

Others will wear her journeys,
put on the skin of her afternoons.

The Fabric-Maker

Wool swings over needles,
exotic rhythms rush along rails.

Firebirds flow through her hands
as she reassembles
old warmths, knits yarns
left from cardigans and gloves,
the family's winters,
lost crimson and scarlet,
snow-velvets,
grey hanks unravelling rain.

For years these oddments have
been stored,
swathes of discarded blue, brown,
remnants of lives,
histories bundled in cupboards.

Genealogy grows in new sleeves,
ghosts and wraiths
spill over her fingers,
there is always
a shade that no one remembers.

We, too, are reworked fabric,
spun in space,
threads from ancient suns,

chemical lace, knitted metals,
iron and phosphorus.
Our veins stream with the heavens,
bones constructed from
the firmament; excavations
from the sky engender the soul.

Grandmother's House

Not a place from shiny magazines
with matched fabrics;

here are clam shells, grasses, wrack,
striated stones,
a branch of driftwood shed
like the sea's antlers,
amber, glass, a piece of silk.

Most artefacts are gifts,
wooden candlesticks carved
by granddad, handmade poppies
from her daughter,
bowl presented by Alice.

A place layered by time and love,
beachcomb colours,
accumulation of offerings from
family and friends,
the small, brass holder chosen
in Benares,
dish made by her son at school,
great-uncle Nelson's
nest of tables and patterned carpet.

Yet the whole has harmony,
a sense of weft,

as if the givers knew
what would settle quietly around her.

Reading the Runes

Grey days spread mosses, lilliputian
ropes over muscle and bone.

She reads the geology under each
visitor's smile,
aware they perceive her eroded,
aged, frail,
forget the lines
on her skin have netted life.

She has inner topography;
charts and maps
for places where she found treasure,
family-skeins,
embroidery of friendships,
networks, distillations,
artefacts made from clunch of love.

Cave-paintings
she alone accomplished,
rich in ochre, umber and heliotrope

Remembering Meg

Rain so pale it leaves
no footprint;

a day of charcoal and pewter,
luminous greys
soft -edged like fur.

She had a dress that texture,
silver in ways
it had been woven
aslant the light,

a birch-bark glitter with
raw silk surfaces,
a hint
of paws placed in soot;

the fabric of dream.

Later, the skirt was made
into cushions,
patches of moonlight
along the sofa,
where like Queen Mab,
she charmed a favourite guest.

For a Friend in Orkney

Seas are ghosts of ancient clouds,
grey-skinned,
they trundle sky, roll its load
of emeralds and marble,
salting the moon.

In the prow of your house
you play Bach,
the small, antique piano releases
each note, a flake of snow;

room fills with unseen shifts,
sounds breaking along
the window, metal so cold
it could bum the skin on a hand.

Outside,
the blizzard is loosely-linked,
mesh so light
it floats upward,
it is the mineral of the music;

drifts accumulating silence
above the abyss,
where cadence is most profound.

Skeining the Rain

Rain: gusts from the wind blew sail over
transparent sail,
nets catching trees, leaves leaping
in shoals like green fish.

We travelled the sea-lanes of streets
to the floating park.
Not for us the house with its anchor
of chairs, battened down
with bulkheads and ballast,
air grounded in rooms like stones.

We broke clouds in pools into
pieces of pewter and tin,
made puzzles in water from willows,
and oaks, thrust arms
through uravelling skeins of sky.

And now,
when the threads between us
are stretched through
distended spaces,
I send my children this day sealed
like a snow-scene
in glass, and hope they will tip up the rain.

Landscape With Rain

In China, they would celebrate rain,
gaze from special pavilions
as it played
over sky and lake and trees.

How it swelled to a huge sail,
its grey embroideries
littered with
silver debris left by light.

Sound-maps;

tintinnabulations from glass-strings
lessened through leaves,
quick spatter along each path,
contours of the garden
revealed as
needles swept like stylos,
cut engravings down slopes of grass.

Each tree has its own rain-song,
pines with crevasses
of silence,
silver-birch spinning tambourines.

We feel its pulse along arteries,
flow with its rhythms and shapes;

whatever our
composition, we are prisms of rain.

The Daughter's Tale

Night-rain: my mother brushing her
long, black hair,
two sounds braiding their silks.

I mourned as she staunched its flow,
stopped light in a knot,
black jewel at the nape of her neck;
my first metamorphosis.

When she combed my hair, tangles
between us gave shocks,
second daughter, not the son
she craved, the boy
who would net a grandmother's love,
redeem my mother's blight
for being the child
who lived, when her brother died.

We all absorb griefs through kin,
have weights that
change an angle in the bones,
crumble tones in a voice,
pull webs through skin.
We take in traumas not our own,
distortions we carry, need not grow.

My mother remained dark water,
a pool, a tarn
that could hold the moon,
but never gave back a reflection
of my light though
I was her dragon-fly, her bird, her fish.

Amber

From England's east coast,
where people
live under mountainous skies,
take on their backs
the full weight of clouds,

it brims in my hand,
yellow stone,
a chunk of cretaceous sun.

It is warm to the touch,
an ember from dusts,
not the ghosts of a life-form
now extinct,
a shift in matter, gold blood.

I have seen necklaces,
great gouts of resin that carry
imprinted forests.

It ripens in my palm,
fossil of an antique afternoon,
distilled wood.

I will give my daughter this lamp
with its freight
of one small sea-creature,
aeons of time;

when she left,
a light went out in the house.

A Taste of Mulberry

I choose for my daughter
this gift
of a plum-coloured shawl,

mulberry fringe,
fantastical
velvet flowers adrift
on deeps, dusks,

spillages of light.

A tactile shade
as found
in certain clarets
and late-medieval glass,

water-rubies,

a fabric
that swallows radiances,
a hue
to reflect in skin;

chiaroscuro,
the art to illumine her face.

Not Jetsam

Old-age love has its own ecstasies:
not autumnal,
not that gold dying,

more like a pebble from England's
east coast,
stippled grey among sea-coal
and amber,
crammed with hidden hues
from the earth, ochres and purples,
rust, rose and burnt umber.

Dull to the casual eye, it holds
pressed fire,
the script from shiftings
within a landscape,
intimations of coral and pearl,
lost tides, moons and tundra spaces.

Weatherings: sun and sea rushing
through veins,
rich ores imprinted by love,
graining from
waves and strata and storms;

piece of creation,
the stuff of the planet;
intangible yet real as pebble or stone.

Letter to Beckie

In September, I met your mother at St Paul's,
the river was silted with skies and the past's remains,
great gulper of junk and jewels, it always enthrals.

Crossed the Millennium Bridge to the Tate. Its halls
were unlovely on the outside, how the light stains
in September. I met your mother. At St Paul's

the stones were white, its tumultuous dome installs
a sense of music. The art gallery entertains,
great gulper of junk and jewels, it always enthrals.

The weather that day was gold and silver squalls.
Laminated with sun and rain in looping skeins,
in September, I met your mother. At St Paul's

we sat on the steps after visiting market stalls,
remembered their glitter set out in little lanes,
great gulpers of junk and jewels. It always enthrals

to cross the river Thames and visit great hauls
of art at the Tate, enjoy its mind-bending gains
in September. I met your mother at St Paul's,
great gulper of history's souls. It always enthrals.

Not the Ordnance Survey

Conversations have maps,
well-marked tracks
for filling gaps in talk,
those emptinesses
that grow like invisible damage
in a room till
we fear something may crack.

Such routes can be learned,
highways, chats
confident in topography,
that offer drinks
and snacks, advice about cars,
hints about garden-centres, facts.

Smaller roads
have fewer charts,
there are hedges to be discerned,
slow speed may be wise,
attention paid
to signs about chicanery,
wild or domestic animals, falling rocks.

At last we enter terra-incognita,
where there may be dragons,
seismology under
smiles can reveal lost worlds

below certain words,
– family, love, friendship, lack –
Who would wish
to disturb a pterodactyl sleeping in
someone's past,
catch sight
of their sabre-toothed tiger?

At the edge of consciousness,
we make our own paths,
here the troll
still lives under skyscrapers,
offices, banks,
here are life-forms not yet born;
the unicorn, demon and angel, the chimera.

Grande Dame

She's a stiffened butterfly pinned to a silk chair
by a pug, her neck encased in a pink frill.
This is no marshmallow lady. She has a flair

for spinning sugar and big, operatic hair,
her confectionery has gone into overkill.
She's a stiffened butterfly. Pinned to a silk chair

she cultivates a delicate, fragile air.
Don't be deceived, there's iron in her will,
this is no marshmallow lady. She has a flair

for being a meringue; there's a tiger in there.
The pretty feathers have steel in every quill.
She's a stiffened butterfly. Pinned to a silk chair,

she uses glamour as camouflage, beware
the carnivore eyes, false lashes in overspill.
This is no marshmallow lady. She has a flair

for the metamorphic smile, is in the snare
of craving to stay young, will pay any bill.
She's a stiffened butterfly pinned to a silk chair
in her ruffles of skin, unable to age with flair.

Apples

Jacob's Strawberry, Permain, Bess Pool,
their ancient recipes lie
coded in wood,
England's old hoards store flavours
from antique weather.

Mature casks of climate,
Ashmeads Kernel, Barnack Beauty, Pippin
ferment our ciderous sun,
rich rain distilled from seas and mist,
hills and trees and grasses.

When thick light strips like velvet
from branches,
I pick my own apples,
rays through leaves
create a green-skinned woman.

Bark-dust falls in my eyes,
insects jangle my hair;
ripping skin on twigs, I reflect on crops,
maids and harvest moons,
the pretty paraphernalia.

Arcadia was always
primed with wounds; Helen, Hesperides, Eden.

Honey

Honey-comb weighted with nectar
of local flowers,
meadow-sweet, campion, clover,
infusions from
dog-rose and vetch.

Its wafer of wax is round
as if for communion,
we take it
reverently on the tongue.

This winter,
outside there are stings,
snow-swarms,
flakes fierce as white bees,

and we
are golden-throated,
spoon long sugars of stopped sun.

Lobster-Fishing at Dawn

Cobbles stretch like a street of huge,
black pearls,
children step to the boat,
smell salt and rope, raw fish.

The sea has drowned some stars,
it seems the Lady of Waves
will raise an enchanted
sword within harbour walls.

They are aware of shabby paint,
scuffed wood,
but this is the ship that flew,
the crew are safe in chain-mail
knitted in rib,
each boathook carries
the sun on its tip like a lance.

They see no mermaid hair
or serpent slain,
but those gigantic claws in pots
might haunt a crack in some
sea-hall and nightly walk its floors.

In the Park

Flowers
are pavement art;

sun crumbles about
us like cake,
we consume light.

Squirrels fizz
with a hint of ginger,
a sherbet lake
spills boats into sky.

Children lug delight
by a limb,

warm fur
to hug in the dark.

Nursery Schools

are crammed with loud, plastic colours
squawking red, yellow, green
and blue,
monsters of the spectrum let loose
like fearsome parrots
amok in corridors and rooms.

Harsh radiations:
head-lamps at full blast that
bruise the spirit,
attack the tender membranes
spinning slow blooms.

No muted gradients fading
light to dusk,
no deeps,
no antique rose or water-silks
that drink sky,
no moons of mood, no hush.

Here, children are cartoons given
hammer-blows of hues;
their heads enclose a mist of
fragile structures
that need to lodge softly

like snow, starlight and stories
and parachuting grasses with migrant seeds.

Mining

Light slipped into sea like icebergs
breaking off Greenland,
big slabs went floating down
to the Humber.

Shale-heaps excavated half the sky,
darkening houses,
stones slipped to the front doors.

Black strata under streets hewn
by each miner's lamp,
a warrior-caste,
men descended from the Vikings.

Larders shone with bilberry, bramble,
blue moons in jars with
a bloom of frost,
bottle-lanterns, brocaded light;
women, too, mined earth.

Children ran on moors in summer,
bracken over their heads,
green cages that climbed the hill,
counterpoint to,
the weight underground
going down through the dark.

Heather loads the land with
purple and blue,
colour-seams, ores to be stored
in the body's bunkers — mined in winter.

White Gardens

Luminous at dusk;

light leaps
towards ice-tinted roses,
is sculpted by
the hydrangea's cool lamps.

A cat with pale fur
blurs
as night settles.

He slips
through green dark amassed
under trees,

light-tarnished,

moves among
sharp-edged aromas,
catmint, thistle,
hot snick of blood in grass,

unlatched,

he sings
to the howling stars,
holds the moon in his mouth.

Creation

This Chinese bowl is
barely tangible,
thin-skinned
as if spun from light.

Poised between
form and disintegration,
it almost breaks
at the edge of vision;

a taut perfection.

We whisper
lest our voices turn
it to dust,
know tenderness at
the passion of its survival.

It's the tremor
we feel when children
in cardboard crowns
tell the Christmas story.

This is the faith;
worked clay defeating death.

Scribing the Iris

The season of Green Rain:

apple-tree buds
appear like drops of water
clinging to
branches after a storm;

raw emeralds,

chandeliers
of grief and remembrance.

March is potent for blue,
the sky
changes its spectrum,
can still
slip through winter-spaces.

Purple was
always your chosen colour.
You loved to embroider
the iris,
as a medieval lady
this would be your device.

Lent
is dark with violets

and absence,
but you
would celebrate creation,

grain of apples in good wood.

Raking the Ancestors

It's not the sifting of towns
I've come to dread,
disturbance of house-bones,
rebuildings
of a civilisation's vertebrae;

it's the graves.

Diggers uncovering fingers,
tops of heads,
a very fine scapula or femur,
handlings;
delight at perfect mandibles,
still hinged.

Despite official tenderness
at grave-goods,
combs and hanks of beads,
cloth, buckles,
pins and phials of glass;

griefs are delicately broken
like a skull,
wreaths of antique flowers
teased apart,
disinterment of tears
displayed like exotic treasure;

a dead child reconstructed on t. v.

The Belhus Script

We walk with a greyhound by the lake,
he is a cadence of movement,
lean, medieval music,
we sense rhythm
in his bones, elisions of skin.

Reeds are in counterpoint aslant
his theme,
grasses orchestrate
a green arrangement of tones,
background sheen
from innumerable textures,
silk and hessian,
dark notes from bulrush and iris.

He flows across staves of leaves;
our fibres like quills
record scrolls along neural paths,
living scripts
we create our own asymmetries
over elemental strings of water and trees.

Amok

Cuttlefish talk through
their skin,

their climate
rolls over a landscape
of flesh,
pulsing pigments make clouds,
each back blazes
with portents, stars.

Does the human brain
converse
with itself using colours,
conjugations of maths
giving Mondrian squares,
love creating mist of a Monet?

Like glow-worms, we use
biology to make light,
minds amok with
unplumbed radar, each body a lamp

Sphere Music

The Tibetan singing bowl
should be
stroked round the rim.

Its circles of sound rise into
the ether
like a potter moulding clay,
distinct as
American Indian smoke-signals
or domes of temples
with their
reverberations in stone.

I'm reminded of Bach,
who turns
wavelengths of light into music,

compositions
now launched into space
to join the flung rings of the spheres.

Jade

Necklace of twenty-four matched
stones from jade
cut with precision pure
as calculus,
like wearing a cool equation mined
from earth's magma.

Green so dense
it draws in the spectator,
the colour of oceans
at certain levels,
as when the sun conjured life,
sharp chemistries
that launched us all on our deeps.

Revered by the Chinese,
its qualities
are reflected in their calligraphy,
brushwork incisive
enough to interpret the Tao.

Precise containment
most displayed by the women,
their lives
the ultimate martial art in self-control.

Walking With Monet

An umbrella with scenes
by Monet
paints Newcastle
in the wet.

Soft panes illumine
your face,
impressionist pavements
lay out your
blue and green path.

Black-velvet beret
aslant
you blaze in
spokes of its spectrum;

irises
raining over
your head, water-lilies
showering light
through a waterproof lake.

Lizzie's First Piece

Learning to play a piece
of music grafts
it in muscle and bone
like a gardener
changing the
grain in fruit or flower.

Music lays down paths;
scales, arpeggios
leaping the synapses create
new ganglia
from codes and maps.

Lullabies transposed into
living tissue,
cortex fashioned from song.

As in quantum-physics,
interchange between wave
and particle,
so the mind leaves physical tracks.

Rose-Petals in Vodka

The book you sent has conjured
an aromatic cloud,
winter-savoury, mint and thyme,
lemon-balm,
jasmine and hedges of box.

Spoors of perfume track
the carpet,
steal into the furnishings,
shock of pine,
lilac, chrysanthemum and phlox.

I could fry flowers from the elder,
steep rose-petals in vodka,
make a still-room,
an arbour, medieval plot of knots.

Balloons of scent will float
their rainbows,
infusions from peonies,
pressings from blue hyssop,
a carnival of shelves
packed with sachets, bottles, pots.

Instead, I plant the seeds
of words,
grow mythic gardens from the stocks.

Kathy's Visits

First, you bring miniature daffodils,
each flower hardly bigger
than a snowflake.

Next it is ornamental eggs
from the east,
every day I imagine a fabled
bird will
hatch into rainbows.

You bring our store of walks
and conversations,
imprintings we share as friends,
spaces, maps;
like scribes we illuminate our
script with grainings
from sedge
and iris, bulrush and reed.

I have seen into other densities,
sky crumbling chalks into
marbled waters, a green-veined lake.

Such resonances
belong to the earth's stillness,
unplayed strings, rain suspended
as white notes;
immanence infusing realities in the skin.

Remembering Easter

Drained by some quality in the light,
visitors drift about like wraiths,
they are trailing ends, threads,
cannot settle in a hospital spectrum.

Like the land of the midnight sun,
the ward is never dark,
the sick laid out
on the snows of their illnesses,
pristine pillows and sheets,
small crevasses between each head.

A place of strange illuminations;
cries at night reducing
sleep to ash, invisible lightnings,
blizzards of confusion.
Pain can blot out awareness of God,
beds are little crosses,
the central-aisle a small via dolorosa.

Does this make sense of part
of the Crucifixion?
Christ crying
"Why hast Thou forsaken me?"
God become human,
God as the sacrifice, not animals or men.

Where else can we take our
fearsome griefs except to the Cross,
its roughcut wood,
blood, despair – the shock of God's love?

Visitation

An aubergine curves above a bowl
in its whale's skin,

pretending
to be a sea-monster,
it swims among earthier beasts,
onion and garlic,
gold coach of a pumpkin.

For a moment I see an ocean,
watch as a fin
progresses among the carrots,

a maverick,

vegetable in a wet-suit,
black satin
show-off spinning lavish light.

Visitation on a bad day;

it circles – bare flanks
fierce, glittering,
more creature at play than threat.

The Dress

Pink velvet with puff sleeves
and rows of tiny buttons,

the child loathed
its shiny smugness, the way
it slopped about her knees,
bodiless as a jellyfish
without the art of swimming.

She liked her brown shorts,
tough cotton, clearly-shaped
with minimum cling,
they reassured her legs
they were
meant to walk fields, hills.

This garment leached her spirit,
it looked feverish, ill,
as it caught
the light and congealed.

Her mother sighed
at the gritted face, sulky dress.
How she had loved the fabric,
its milky sheen now soured,
fit only to be
mopped up by its
tissue-paper wrapping, laid to rest.

Pumping Iron

Blacksmiths inhabit my family-tree,
men trained
to shape the guts of the world,
swords and ploughshares,
rivets, nails,
wheels on carts and carriages.

Did they love the horses they shod,
prefer massive shires
to the more delicate hunters?

My notion of their lives is smudged
by warm, Victorian paintings,
'AT THE FORGE',
earth-colours, sunny and cosy,
a porcelain child at the door.

And all that mystical stuff, did my kin
feel reverberations?
How the gods loved armourers,
martial-arts, soul minerals
poured into metals,
myths forged from the ores
in our heads – Excalibur, Wayland.

And now I'm hammering words
to the hooves of language,
send them galloping across the page.

Second Sight

She takes colour-soundings
under trees,
fox-lamps fermenting
brown sugars,

the landscape
crumbles like gingerbread.

Removal of cataracts disturbs
in a rich,
Hitchcockian way,
no pain,
men in masks,
echoes from medical gothic.

Patients
came from five cultures,
all immersed
in the same spectrum;

grew micro-language.

And after shocks re-learning
old ghost-colours,
(chair yellow not brown,
  jumper pink not red),
the world emerges
from tissues of everlasting rain.

Each dawn
the room has that special
clarity that
comes from overnight snow;

she looks for the terracotta sun.

Acknowledgements continued

Prizes

'The Fabric-Maker' won first prize in the Split the Lark Competition; 'Lobster Fishing at Staithes' won first prize in the Crabbe Memorial Competition; 'Amber' won first prize in the Wymondham Poetry Festival; 'Skeining the Rain' won first prize in the Sefton Poetry Competition; 'White Gardens' won second prize in the Border's Bookshop Competition; 'Assembling the Yarn' won second prize in the York Poetry Competition, 2005; 'Woman Knitting' won third prize in the Lincoln 'Help the Aged' Poetry Competition; 'Before Lazarus' won third prize in the Manchester Cathedral Poetry Competition; 'Not the Ordnance Survey' was awarded a £100 prize in the A.E. Housman Memorial Competition.

Printed in the United Kingdom
by Lightning Source UK Ltd.
122575UK00001B/130-150/A